In the Year 1978

by

Kerry Butters.

In the Year 1978

Millennium: 2nd millennium

Centuries: 19th century – **20th century** – 21st century

Decades: 1940s 1950s 1960s – **1970s** – 1980s 1990s 2000s

Years: 1975 1976 1977 – **1978** – 1979 1980 1981

1978 (MCMLXXVIII) was a common year starting on Sunday (dominical letter A) of the Gregorian calendar, the 1978th year of the Common Era (CE) and *Anno Domini* (AD) designations, the 978th year of the 2nd millennium, the 78th year of the 20th century, and the 9th year of the 1970s decade.

Contents

Events

January

- January 1
  - The Copyright Act of 1976 takes effect, making sweeping changes to United States copyright law.
  - Air India Flight 855, a Boeing 747 passenger jet, crashes into the ocean near Bombay, killing 213.
  - Edward M. Davis retires from the Los Angeles Police Department after 30 years on the force and more than 8 years as its police chief.
- January 4 – A referendum in Chile supports the policies of dictator Augusto Pinochet (see Chilean national consultation, 1978).
- January 5 – Bülent Ecevit, of CHP forms the new government of Turkey (42nd government).
- January 6 – The Holy Crown of Hungary (also known as Stephen of Hungary Crown) is returned to Hungary from the United States, where it was held since World War II.
- January 10 – Pedro Joaquín Chamorro Cardenal, a critic of the Nicaraguan government, is assassinated; riots erupt against Somoza's government.
- January 14 – January 15 – The body of former U.S. Vice President Hubert Humphrey lies in state in the Capitol Rotunda, following his death from cancer.
- January 16 – Robert F. Rock succeeds Edward M. Davis as LAPD's interim chief.

- January 18 – The European Court of Human Rights finds the British government guilty of mistreating prisoners in Northern Ireland, but not guilty of torture.
- January 19 – Federal Appeals Court Judge William H. Webster is appointed FBI Director.
- January 22 – Ethiopia declares the ambassador of West Germany persona non grata.
- January 24
  - Soviet satellite Kosmos 954 burns up in Earth's atmosphere, scattering debris over Canada's Northwest Territories.
  - Rose Dugdale and Eddie Gallagher become the first convicted prisoners to marry in prison in the history of the Republic of Ireland.
- January 25 – January 27 – The Great Blizzard of 1978 strikes the Ohio Valley and Great Lakes, killing 70.
- January 28 – Richard Chase, the "Vampire of Sacramento", is arrested.

February

- February 1 – Hollywood film director Roman Polanski skips bail and flees to France, after pleading guilty to charges of engaging in sex with a 13-year-old girl.
- February 5 – February 7 – The Northeastern United States blizzard of 1978 hits the New England region and the New York metropolitan area, killing about 100 and causing over US$520 million in damage.
- February 6 – King Dragon operation in Arakan: Burmese General Ne Win targets Muslim minorities in the village of Sakkipara.
- February 8 – United States Senate proceedings are broadcast on radio for the first time.
- February 8 – Project SHAWN begins in Connecticut.
- February 11
  - Pacific Western Airlines Flight 314, a Boeing 737-200, crashes in Cranbrook, British Columbia, killing 44 of the 50 people on board.

- ○ Sixteen Unification Church couples wed in New York City.
  - ○ Somalia mobilizes its troops, due to an apparent Ethiopian attack.
  - ○ The People's Republic of China lifts a ban on works by Aristotle, William Shakespeare and Charles Dickens.
- February 13 – Sydney Hilton Hotel bombing: A bomb explodes outside the Hilton Hotel in Sydney, Australia, killing 2 garbagemen, a policeman and injuring several others.
- February 15
  - ○ Rhodesia, one of only two remaining white-ruled African nations (the other being South Africa), announces that it will accept multiracial democracy within 2 years.
  - ○ Serial killer Ted Bundy is captured in Pensacola, Florida.
- February 16
  - ○ The Hillside Strangler, a serial killer prowling Los Angeles, claims a tenth and final victim.
  - ○ The first computer bulletin board system (*CBBS*) is created in Chicago.
- February 19 – Egyptian raid on Larnaca International Airport
- February 21 – Electrical workers in Mexico City find the remains of the Great Pyramid of Tenochtitlan in the middle of the city.

March

- March 1 – Charlie Chaplin's remains are stolen from Cosier-sur-Vevey, Switzerland.
- March 2 – *Soyuz 28* (Aleksei Gubarev, Vladimír Remek) is launched on a rendezvous with *Salyut 6*, with the first cosmonaut from a third country (besides the Soviet Union and United States) – Czechoslovak citizen Vladimír Remek.
- March 3
  - ○ Ethiopia admits that its troops are fighting with the aid of Cuban soldiers against Somalian troops in the Ogaden.
  - ○ Rhodesia attacks Zambia.

- o The *New York Post* publishes an article about David Rorvik's book *The Cloning of Man*, about a supposed cloning of a human being.
- March 5 – Wuthering Heights the debut single by Kate Bush charts at #1 making her the first woman to have a self-penned number one single.
- March 6 – American porn publisher Larry Flynt is shot and paralyzed in Lawrenceville, Georgia.
- March 10 – *Soyuz 28* lands.
- March 11 – Coastal Road massacre: Palestinian terrorists kill 34 Israelis.
- March 14 – Operation Litani: Israeli forces invade Lebanon.
- March 15 – Somalia and Ethiopia sign a truce to end the Ethio-Somali War.
- March 16 – Former Italian Premier Aldo Moro is kidnapped by the Red Brigades; 5 bodyguards are killed.
- March 17 – The oil tanker *Amoco Cadiz* runs aground on the coast of Brittany.
- March 18
  - o Zulfikar Ali Bhutto, Prime Minister of Pakistan, is sentenced to death by hanging for ordering the assassination of a political opponent.
  - o California Jam II is held at the Ontario Motor Speedway in Ontario, California, attracting more than 300,000 fans.
- March 22 – Karl Wallenda of The Flying Wallendas dies after falling off a tight-rope between two hotels in San Juan, Puerto Rico.
- March 26 – The control tower and some other facilities of New Tokyo International Airport, which were scheduled to open on March 31, are illegally occupied and damaged in a terrorist attack by New Left activists, forcing a rescheduling of its opening date to May 20.
- March 28
  - o San Francisco city council signs the U.S.'s most comprehensive homosexual rights bill.

- *Stump v. Sparkman* (435 U.S. 349): The Supreme Court of the United States hands down a 5–3 decision in a controversial case involving involuntary sterilization and judicial immunity.
- Daryl Gates succeeds Robert F. Rock as LAPD's chief, a role he will keep for the next 14 years.

April

- April 1
  - New Zealand National Airways Corporation (the domestic airline of New Zealand) is merged with New Zealand's international airline, Air New Zealand.
  - Dick Smith of Dick Smith Foods tows a fake iceberg to Sydney Harbour.
  - The Philippine College of Commerce, through a presidential decree, is converted to the Polytechnic University of the Philippines.
- April 2 – Dallas debuted on CBS and gave birth to the modern day primetime soap opera.
- April 3 – The 50th Academy Awards are held at the Dorothy Chandler Pavilion in Los Angeles with *Annie Hall* winning Best Picture.
- April 7 – U.S. President Jimmy Carter decides to postpone production of the neutron bomb – a weapon which kills people with radiation but leaves buildings relatively intact.
- April 8 – Regular radio broadcasts of British Parliament proceedings start.
- April 9 – Somali military officers stage an unsuccessful coup against the government of Siad Barre; security forces thwart the attempt within hours, and several conspirators are arrested.
- April 10 – Volkswagen becomes the second (after Rolls-Royce) non-American automobile manufacturer to open a plant in the United States, commencing production of the Rabbit, the North American version of the Volkswagen Golf, at the Volkswagen

Westmoreland Assembly Plant near New Stanton, Pennsylvania with a unionized (UAW) workforce (the plant closes in 1992).

- April 14 – 1978 Tbilisi Demonstrations: Thousands of Georgians demonstrate against an attempt by Soviet authorities to change the constitutional status of the Georgian language.
- April 18 – The U.S. Senate votes 68–32 to turn the Panama Canal over to Panamanian control on December 31, 1999.
- April 20 – Soviet air defense shot down Korean Air Lines Flight 902. The plane made an emergency landing on a frozen lake.
- April 22

Afghanistan President Daoud Khan was assassinated by the People's Democratic Party of Afghanistan on April 25

-
  - Izhar Cohen & the Alphabeta win the Eurovision Song Contest 1978 for Israel with their song "A-Ba-Ni-Bi".
  - The One Love Peace Concert is held at National Heroes Stadium in Kingston, Jamaica. Bob Marley unites 2 opposing political leaders at this concert, bringing peace to the civil war-ridden streets of the city.
- April 25 – St. Paul, Minnesota becomes the second U.S. city to repeal its gay rights ordinance after Anita Bryant's successful 1977 anti-gay campaign in Dade County, Florida.
- April 27 – Afghanistan President Daoud Khan is killed during a military coup; Nur Muhammad Taraki succeeds him beginning the Afghan Civil War which as of 2014 has not ended.
- April 30 – The Democratic Republic of Afghanistan is proclaimed under pro-communist leader Nur Muhammad Taraki.

May

- May 4
  - The Battle of Cassinga occurs in southern Angola.
  - Communist activist Henri Curiel is murdered in Paris.
- May 5 – Pete Rose of the Cincinnati Reds gets his 3,000th major league hit.
- May 8
  - Norway opens a natural gas field in the Polar Sea.
  - Reinhold Messner (Italy) and Peter Habeler (Austria) make the first ascent of Mount Everest without supplemental oxygen.
- May 9 – In Rome, the corpse of former Italian prime minister Aldo Moro is found in a red Renault 4.
- May 12 – In Zaire, rebels occupy the city of Kolwezi, the mining centre of the province of Shaba. The Zairean government asks the U.S., France and Belgium to restore order.
- May 12 – May 13 – A group of mercenaries led by Bob Denard oust Ali Soilih in the Comoros; 10 local soldiers are killed. Denard forms a new government.
- May 15
  - Australia's longest serving prime minister sir Robert Menzies dies.
  - Students of the University of Tehran riot in Tabriz; the army stops the riot.
- May 17 – Charlie Chaplin's coffin is found some 15 km from the cemetery from which it was stolen, near Lake Geneva.
- May 18
  - Soviet dissident Yuri Orlov is sentenced to 7 years hard labor for distributing 'counterrevolutionary material'.
  - Sarajevo is selected to host the 1984 Winter Olympics and Los Angeles is selected to host the 1984 Summer Olympics.
- May 18 – May 19 – Belgian and French paratroopers fly to Zaire to aid the fight against the rebels.
- May 19 – May 20 – French Foreign Legion paratroopers land in Kolwezi, Zaire, to rescue Europeans in the middle of a civil war.

- May 20 – Mavis Hutchinson, 53, becomes the first woman to run across the U.S.; her trek took 69 days.
- May 22 – Exiled leaders Ahmed Abdallah and Muhammad Ahmad return to the Comoros.
- May 25 – A bomb explodes in the security section of Northwestern University, wounding a security guard (the first Unabomber attack).
- May 26 – In Atlantic City, New Jersey, Resorts International, the first legal casino in the eastern United States, opens.
- May 28 – Indianapolis 500: Al Unser wins his third race, and the first for car owner Jim Hall.
- May 29 – Ali Soilih is found dead in the Comoros, allegedly shot when trying to escape.

June

- June 1 – The 1978 FIFA World Cup starts in Argentina.
- June 3 – The Congo Republic recognizes the Sahrawi Arab Democratic Republic (SADR).
- June 6 – California voters approve Proposition 13, which slashes property taxes nearly 60%.
- June 9 – The Church of Jesus Christ of Latter-day Saints extends the priesthood and temple blessings to "all worthy males", ending a general policy of excluding "Canaanites" from priesthood ordination and temple ordinances.
- June 12 – Serial killer David Berkowitz, the "Son of Sam," is sentenced to 365 years in prison.
- June 15 – King Hussein of Jordan marries 26-year-old Lisa Halaby, who takes the name Queen Noor.
- June 16 – *Grease*, starring John Travolta and Olivia Newton-John is released.
- June 19
  - Cricketer Ian Botham becomes the first man in the history of the game to score a century and take 8 wickets in 1 inning of a Test match.

- o *Garfield*, which eventually becomes the world's most widely syndicated comic strip, makes its debut.
- June 20 – A magnitude 6.5 earthquake hits Thessaloniki, Greece's second largest city, killing 45 people, injuring hundreds and damaging some of the city's Byzantine landmarks.
- June 21
  - o A shootout between Provisional IRA members and the British Army leaves 1 civilian and 3 IRA men dead.
  - o 1978 Iranian Chinook shootdown: Iranian helicopters stray into Soviet airspace and are shot down.
- June 22
  - o Charon, a satellite of Pluto, is discovered.
  - o São Tomé and Príncipe recognizes the Sahrawi Arab Democratic Republic (SADR).
- June 23 – Panama recognizes the Sahrawi Arab Democratic Republic (SADR).
- June 24
  - o Yemen Arab Republic President Ahmad al-Ghashmi is killed.
  - o The Gay & Lesbian Solidarity March is held in Sydney, Australia to mark the 10th Anniversary of the Stonewall riots (which later becomes the annual Sydney Gay and Lesbian Mardi Gras; later incorporating a festival).
- June 25 – Argentina defeats the Netherlands 3–1 after extra time to win the 1978 FIFA World Cup.
- June 26 – A bombing by Breton nationalists causes destruction in Palace of Versailles.
- June 28
  - o The U.S. scientific satellite Seasat is launched.
  - o *University of California Regents v. Bakke*: The Supreme Court of the United States bars quota systems in college admissions but affirms the constitutionality of programs which give advantages to minorities.
- June 30 – Ethiopia begins a massive offensive in Eritrea.

July

- July 3 – The Amazon Co-operation Treaty (ACT) is signed.
- July 7 – The Solomon Islands become independent from the United Kingdom.
- July 11 – More than 200 tourists die in an explosion of a tanker-truck at a campsite in Costa Daurada, Spain.
- July 25
    - Cerro Maravilla murders: Two Puerto Rican pro-independence activists are killed in a police ambush.
    - Louise Brown, the world's first test tube baby, is born in Oldham, Greater Manchester, UK.

August

- August 6 – Pope Paul VI dies in Castel Gandolfo.
- August 17 – Double Eagle II becomes the first balloon to successfully cross the Atlantic Ocean, flying from Presque Isle, Maine, to Miserey, France.
- August 19 – Birth of Omani entrepreneur Qais Al Khonji
- August 22 – Sandinistas seize the Nicaraguan National Palace.
- August 26 – Pope John Paul I succeeds Pope Paul VI as the 263rd Pope.

September

September 6: Anwar Sadat, Jimmy Carter, and Menachem Begin meet on the Aspen Cabin patio at Camp David.

- September 3 – Annual Urs sharif of Gulam Ghous Qadri Sadikshah baba (R. A.) Maharashtra.
- September 5 – Camp David Accords: Menachem Begin and Anwar Sadat begin the peace process at Camp David, Maryland.
- September 7
  - In London, England, a poison-filled pellet, supposedly injected using an umbrella, poisons Bulgarian defector Georgi Markov, probably on orders of Bulgarian intelligence; he dies 4 days later.
  - In London, England, Keith Moon dies in Curzon Place, Mayfair.
- September 8 – Iranian Army troops open fire on rioters in Tehran, killing 122, wounding 4,000.
- September 16
  - General Muhammad Zia-ul-Haq officially assumes the post of President of Pakistan.
  - The 7.4 Mw Tabas earthquake affects the city of Tabas, Iran with a maximum Mercalli intensity of IX (Violent). At least 15,000 people were killed.
- September 17 – The Camp David Accords are signed between Israel and Egypt.
- September 19 – Police in the West Midlands of England launch a massive murder hunt, when 13-year-old newspaper boy Carl Bridgewater is shot dead after disturbing a burglary.
- September 20 – General Rahimuddin Khan assumes the post of Martial Law Governor of Balochistan.
- September 25
  - PSA Flight 182, a Boeing 727, collides with a small private airplane and crashes in San Diego, California; 144 are killed.
  - Giuseppe Verdi's opera *Otello* makes its first appearance on *Live from the Met*, in a complete production of the opera starring Jon Vickers. This is the first complete television broadcast of the opera in the U.S. since the historic 1948 one.
- September 27 – The last Forest Brother guerrilla movement fighter is discovered and killed in Estonia.
- September 28 – Pope John Paul I dies after only 33 days of papacy.

October

- October 1
  - Vietnam attacks Cambodia.
  - Tuvalu becomes independent from the United Kingdom.
- October 7 – *Wranslide* in New South Wales: the Wran government is re-elected with an increased majority.
- October 8 – Australia's Ken Warby sets the current world water speed record of 317.6 mph (511.13 km/h) at Blowering Dam, Australia.
- October 10
  - Daniel arap Moi becomes president of Kenya.
  - A massive short circuit in Seasat's electrical system ends the satellite's scientific mission.
  - United States President Jimmy Carter signs a bill that authorizes the minting of the Susan B. Anthony dollar.
- October 13 – The Soviet Union launches a major Russification campaign throughout all union republics.
- October 14
  - U.S. President Jimmy Carter signs a bill into law which allows homebrewing of beer in the United States.
- October 16 – Pope John Paul II succeeds Pope John Paul I as the 264th pope, resulting in the first Year of Three Popes since 1605. He is the first Polish pope in history, and the first non-Italian pope since Pope Adrian VI (1522–1523).
- October 18 – Thorbjörn Fälldin steps down as Prime Minister of Sweden, and is succeeded by the Leader of the liberal People's Party (*"Folkpartiet"*) Ola Ullsten.
- October 20 – The first Sydney Gay and Lesbian Mardi Gras is held as a protest march and commemoration of the Stonewall riots.
- October 21 – Australian civilian pilot Frederick Valentich vanishes in a Cessna 182 over the Bass Strait south of Melbourne, after reporting contact with an unidentified aircraft.
- October 27 – Egyptian President Anwar Sadat and Israeli Prime Minister Menachem Begin win the Nobel Peace Prize for their progress toward achieving a Middle East accord.

November

- November 2: 8:00 pm – The Republic of Ireland's second television channel RTÉ 2 goes on air (renamed Network 2, 1988; RTÉ Network Two, 1995; N2, 1997; and RTÉ Two in 2004).
- November 3
  - Dominica gains its independence from the United Kingdom.
  - Equatorial Guinea recognizes the Sahrawi Arab Democratic Republic (SADR).
- November 5 – Rioters sack the British Embassy in Tehran.
- November 7
  - Indira Gandhi is re-elected to the Indian parliament.
  - California voters defeat the Briggs Initiative that would have prohibited gay school teachers.
- November 9 – Tanzania recognizes the Sahrawi Arab Democratic Republic (SADR).
- November 18 – Jonestown incident: In Guyana, Jim Jones leads his Peoples Temple cult in a mass murder–suicide that claims 918 lives in all, 909 of them at Jonestown itself, including over 270 children. Congressman Leo J. Ryan is assassinated by members of Peoples Temple shortly beforehand.
- November 19 – The first U.S. Take Back the Night march occurs in San Francisco.
- November 27 – In San Francisco, Mayor George Moscone and City Supervisor Harvey Milk are assassinated by former Supervisor Dan White.
- November 30 – Publication of *The Times* is suspended due to labor problems until November 13, 1979.

December

- December 4 – Dianne Feinstein succeeds the murdered George Moscone, to become the first woman mayor of San Francisco (she serves until January 8, 1988).
- December 6 – The Spanish Constitution officially restores the country's democratic government.
-

- December 11
  - Lufthansa heist: Six men rob a Lufthansa cargo facility in New York City's John F. Kennedy International Airport.
  - Two million demonstrate against the Shah in Iran.
- December 13 – The first Susan B. Anthony dollars were struck at the Philadelphia Mint.
- December 15
  - Cleveland, Ohio becomes the first major American city to go into default since the Great Depression, under Mayor Dennis Kucinich.
  - *Superman* is released in cinemas in the United States.
- December 16 – Train 87 from Nanjing to Xining collides with train 368 from Xi'an to Xuzhou near Yangzhuang railway station in China, killing 106, injuring 218.
- December 19 – Former Prime Minister of India Indira Gandhi is arrested and jailed for a week for breach of privilege and contempt of parliament.
- December 22
  - The pivotal Third Plenum of the 11th National Congress of the Communist Party of China is held in Beijing, with Deng Xiaoping reversing Mao-era policies to pursue a program for Chinese economic reform.
  - Chicago serial killer John Wayne Gacy, who was subsequently convicted of the murder of 33 young men and boys between 1972 and 1978, is arrested.
  - Argentina started the Operation Soberanía against Chile.
- December 25 – Vietnam launches a major offensive against the Khmer Rouge of Cambodia.
- December 27 – The Constitution of Spain is approved in a referendum, officially ending 40 years of military dictatorship.

Date unknown

- Artificial insulin is invented.
- David Rorvik claims he has participated in a creation of a human clone in his book *In His Image*.
- Abortion is legalized in Italy for the first time.
- In Seoul, Korea, construction begins on Seoul Subway Line 2.
- Ford initiates a recall for the Pinto because of a public outcry resulting from deaths associated with gas tank explosions.
- The New York International Bible Society's New International Version of the complete *Holy Bible* translated into modern American English is published.
- The Soviet Union nuclear weapons stockpile exceeds the United States nuclear weapons stockpile.

Births

January

Karina Smirnoff

Sheamus

- January 1
  - Philip Mulryne, Northern Irish footballer
  - Vidya Balan, Bollywood actress
- January 2
  - Megumi Toyoguchi, Japanese voice actress
  - Karina Smirnoff, Ukrainian dancer
- January 3
  - Kimberley Locke, American singer and model
  - Liya Kebede, Ethiopian model, clothing designer and actress
  - Park Sol-mi, South Korean actress
- January 4 – Karine Ruby, French snowboarder (d. 2009)
- January 5 – Franck Montagny, French Formula One driver
- January 7 – Emilio Palma, Argentine citizen, first human born in Antarctica
- January 9
  - Chad Ocho Cinco, American football player
  - A. J. McLean, American singer (Backstreet Boys)
- January 10 – Kanako Mitsuhashi, Japanese voice actress
- January 11 – Emile Heskey, English football player
- January 13
  - Nate Silver, American statistician, sabermetrician, psephologist, and writer.
  - Ashmit Patel, Indian actor
- January 14 – Shawn Crawford, American runner
- January 15
  - Eddie Cahill, American actor
  - Franco Pellizotti, Italian professional road racing cyclist
- January 18 – Katja Kipping, German politician
- January 19 – Bamboo Mañalac, Filipino musician and singer
- January 24
  - Nami Miyahara, Japanese voice actress, singer
  - Mark Hildreth, Canadian actor/voice actor
- January 25 – Gordie Dwyer American former NHL player and coach
- January 26 – Kelly Stables, American actress
-

- January 28
  - Gianluigi Buffon, Italian goalkeeper (football)
  - Jamie Carragher, English footballer
  - Sheamus, Irish professional wrestler
- January 31 – Ibolya Oláh, Hungarian singer

February

Ashton Kutcher

Omotola Jalade Ekeinde

- February 2
  - Barry Ferguson, Scottish footballer
  - Guido Kaczka, Argentine television show host and actor
- February 5
  - Brian Russell, American football player
  - Samuel Sánchez, Spanish road bicycle racer
  -

- February 7
  - Ashton Kutcher, American actor (*That '70s Show*)
  - Omotola Jalade Ekeinde, Nigerian actress, singer, philanthropist and former model
- February 12
  - Gethin Jones, British (Welsh) television presenter
  - Silver Meikar, Estonian politician
- February 13 – Niklas Bäckström, Finnish hockey player (Minnesota Wild)
- February 14
  - Richard Hamilton, American basketball player
  - Darius Songaila, Lithuanian basketball player
- February 15 – Tuan Le, American poker player
- February 16
  - John Tartaglia, American Broadway actor and Muppeteer
  - Tia Hellebaut, Belgian athlete
- February 17 – Jacob Wetterling, American child kidnapping victim (missing since 1989)
- February 18 – Oliver Pocher, German actor, stand-up comedian and television host
- February 19
  - Kenyatta Wright, American football linebacker
  - Immortal Technique, Peruvian-born American rapper
- February 20 – Julia Jentsch, German actress
- February 21 – Kumail Nanjiani, Pakistani-American actor and comedian
- February 22 – Jenny Frost, English singer (Atomic Kitten)
- February 23 – Dan Snyder, Canadian hockey player (d. 2003)
- February 24
  - Leon Constantine, British Leeds United footballer
  - Gary, South Korean musician, entertainer
- February 27 – Kakha Kaladze, Georgian and A.C. Milan footballer
- February 28
  - Benjamin Raich, Austrian Olympic skier
  - Jeanne Cherhal, French singer-songwriter
  - Yasir Hameed, Pakistani cricketer

March

Jaqueline Jesus

Claudio Sanchez

Pieter van den Hoogenband

Jensen Ackles

- March 1
  - Jensen Ackles, American actor
  - Donovan Patton, Guamanian television star
  - Sakura Nogawa, Japanese voice actress
- March 2 – Tomáš Kaberle, Czech hockey player
- March 4 – Denis Dallan, Italian rugby union footballer
- March 6
  - Sage Rosenfels, American football player
  - Mike Jackson, American politician
- March 7 – Jaqueline Jesus, Brazilian psychologist and activist
- March 8 – Mohammed Bouyeri, Dutch mobster, murderer of Theo van Gogh
- March 10 – Benjamin Burnley, American musician (Breaking Benjamin)
- March 11 – Didier Drogba, Ivorian footballer
- March 12
  - Neal Obermeyer, American editorial cartoonist
  - Claudio Sanchez, American writer and musician
- March 13
  - Tom Danielson, American cyclist
  - Kenny Watson, American football player
- March 14
  - Pieter van den Hoogenband, Dutch swimmer
  - Carl Johan Bergman, Swedish biathlete
  - Moon Hee-joon, Korean singer
- March 15 – Flavio Furtado, Cape Verdean boxer
- March 17
  - Jason M. Burns, American writer
  - Patrick Seitz, American voice actor
- March 19 – Ilmur Kristjánsdóttir, Icelandic actress
- March 20 – Roel van Velzen, Dutch Musician
- March 21 – Rani Mukerji, Indian actress
- March 22 – Josh Heupel, American football player
- March 23
  - Simon Gärdenfors, Swedish cartoonist and radio host
  - Nicholle Tom, American actress

- March 29 – Igor Rakočević, Serbian basketball player
- March 31
  - Stephen Clemence, English footballer
  - Jérôme Rothen, French footballer

April

Duncan James

John Smit

James Franco

Stana Katic

- April 1
    - Vitor Belfort, Brazilian martial artist
    - Antonio de Nigris, Mexican footballer (d. 2009)
- April 2 – Nick Berg, American businessman (d. 2004)
- April 3
    - Matthew Goode, English actor
    - John Smit, South African rugby union player
- April 4
    - Jason Ellison, American baseball player
    - Sam Moran, Australian singer and former member of The Wiggles
    - Irene Skliva, Miss World 1996
- April 5 – Franziska van Almsick, German swimmer
- April 6 – Tim Hasselbeck, American football player
- April 7 – Duncan James, English singer (Blue)
- April 9
    - Jorge Andrade, Portuguese footballer
    - Rachel Stevens, English singer (S Club 7)
    - Veronica Taylor, American voice actress
- April 12
    - Cheeming Boey, Malaysian artist
    - Guy Berryman, Scottish musician
- April 13 – Kyle Howard, American television and movie actor
-

- April 16
  - Matthew Lloyd, Australian rules footballer
  - Lara Dutta, Indian actress and Miss Universe 2000
- April 17
  - Jason White, Scottish rugby union player
  - Juan Guillermo Castillo, Uruguayan goalkeeper
- April 19 – James Franco, American actor
- April 20
  - Mirei Kuroda, Japanese gravure idol
  - Matt Austin, Canadian actor
- April 21 – Jukka Nevalainen, Finnish drummer (Nightwish)
- April 23 – Princess Tamara Czartoryski-Borbon, Spanish athlete
- April 25 – Duncan Kibet, Kenyan long-distance runner
- April 26 – Stana Katic, American actress
- April 28
  - Nate Richert, American musician and former actor
  - Robert Oliveri, American former actor

May

Ricardo Carvalho

Kenan Thompson

David Krumholtz

- May 1 – James Badge Dale, American actor
- May 3
  - Lawrence Tynes, American football player
  - Autumn Phillips, British wife of Peter Phillips, son of Anne, Princess Royal
- May 4
  - Erin Andrews, American ESPN personality
  - Daisuke Ono, Japanese voice actor
- May 6 – Aleksandr Fyodorov, Russian bodybuilder
- May 7
  - Brian Clevinger, American author
  - Shawn Marion, American basketball player
  -

- May 10
  - Kenan Thompson, American actor (*Saturday Night Live*)
  - Marcelo Moretto, Brazilian footballer
- May 11 – Laetitia Casta, French supermodel and actress
- May 12
  - Hossein Rezazadeh, Iranian weightlifter
  - Jason Biggs, American actor
  - Aya Ishiguro, Japanese singer, writer, and fashion designer
  - Malin Åkerman, Swedish-Canadian Actress
- May 13
  - Mike Bibby, American basketball player
  - Barry Zito, American baseball player
- May 15
  - Caroline Dhavernas, French-Canadian actress
  - Dwayne De Rosario, Canadian footballer
  - David Krumholtz, American actor
  - Krissy Taylor, American model (d. 1995)
  - Krzysztof Ignaczak, Polish volleyball player
- May 17 – Kat Foster, American actress
- May 18 – Ricardo Carvalho, Portuguese footballer
- May 19 – Marcus Bent, English footballer
- May 21
  - Adam Gontier, lead singer of Canadian band Three Days Grace
  - Briana Banks, German-American porn star
- May 22
  - Katie Price (Jordan), English model and television personality
  - Ginnifer Goodwin, American actress
- May 23
  - Scott Raynor, Drummer and founding member of Blink-182
  - Carolyn Moos, American model and professional basketball player
- May 25 – Brian Urlacher, American football player
- May 26 – Benji Gregory, former American actor
-

- May 29
  - Lorenzo Odone, American adrenoleukodystrophy patient (d. 2008)
  - Adam Rickitt, English actor, singer and model

June

Bill Hader

Daniel Brühl

Mía Maestro

Zoe Saldana

Frank Lampard

Dan Wheldon

Nicole Scherzinger

- June 1
  - Antonietta Di Martino, Italian high-jumper
  - Link Neal, American musician, comedian and internet personality, host of "Good Mythical Morning"
- June 2
  - Nikki Cox, American actress
  - Justin Long, American actor
- June 4
  - Simone Maludrottu, Italian boxer
  - Robin Lord Taylor, American actor
- June 5 – Nick Kroll, American actor and comedian
- June 6
  - Judith Barsi, American child actress (d. 1988)
  - Carl Barât, English musician
  - Mariana Popova, Bulgarian singer

- June 7
  - Jesse Ball, American novelist and poet
  - Bill Hader, American actor (*Saturday Night Live*)
- June 8 – Maria Menounos, American actress, journalist, and television presenter
- June 9
  - Michaela Conlin, American actress
  - Shandi Finnessey, American model and actress, Miss USA 2004
  - Miroslav Klose, German professional footballer
  - Matthew Bellamy, British multi-instrumentalist and singer (Muse)
- June 10
  - Shane West, American actor
  - Han Hee-won, South Korean golfer
  - Karl Scully, Irish tenor
- June 11 – Joshua Jackson, Canadian actor
- June 15
  - Wilfred Bouma, Dutch football player
  - Anna Torv, Australian actress
- June 16 – Daniel Brühl, German actor
- June 18 – Tara Platt American voice actress/actress
- June 19
  - Dirk Nowitzki, German basketball player
  - Mía Maestro, Argentine actress
  - Zoe Saldana, American actress
  - Garfield, fictional character from the *Garfield* comic strip
- June 20
  - Quinton Jackson, American mixed martial arts fighter
  - Frank Lampard, English footballer
- June 21
  - Erica Durance, Canadian actress
  - Jean-Pascal Lacoste, French singer, actor and TV host
- June 22
  - Champ Bailey, American football player
  - Dan Wheldon, English race car driver (d. 2011)

- o Tim Driesen, Belgian actor and singer-songwriter
- June 24
  - o Ariel Pink, American indie rock musician
  - o Emppu Vuorinen, Finnish rock musician (Nightwish)
  - o Juan Román Riquelme, Argentine football player
  - o Shunsuke Nakamura, Japanese football player
- June 25
  - o Aftab Shivdasani, Indian actor
  - o Marcus Stroud, American football player
  - o Layla El, British wrestler
  - o Aramis Ramírez, Dominican baseball player
- June 27 – Anna Kumble, English pop singer and TV presenter
- June 28 – Ha Ji-won, South Korean actress and singer
- June 29 – Nicole Scherzinger, American pop singer (The Pussycat Dolls)
- June 30
  - o Ben Cousins, Australian rules footballer
  - o Pat Dennis, American football player

July

Topher Grace

Michelle Rodriguez

Pavel Datsyuk

Josh Hartnett

- July 1 – Hillary Tuck, American actress
- July 2 – Diana Gurtskaya, blind Georgian singer
- July 3 – Mizuki Noguchi, Japanese long-distance runner
- July 4
  - Tony Reali, American sports personality
  - Becki Newton, American actress
- July 6
  - Kevin Senio, New Zealand rugby union footballer
  - Tia and Tamera Mowry, African-American actresses

- July 8 – Rachael Lillis, American actress
- July 9
  - Linda Park, Korean-born actress
  - Mark Medlock, German pop singer (*Deutschland sucht den Superstar*'s Season 4)
- July 10 – Jesse Lacey, American singer-songwriter
- July 12
  - Bradley Eustace, Australian composer
  - Topher Grace, American actor (*That '70s Show*)
  - Michelle Rodriguez, American actress
- July 15 – Greg Sestero, French-American actor and model
- July 17 – Panda Bear, American musician
- July 18
  - Shane Horgan, Irish rugby player
  - Virginia Raggi, Italian lawyer, Mayor of Rome
  - Ben Sheets, American baseball player
- July 20
  - Pavel Datsyuk, Russian ice hockey player
  - Charlie Korsmo, American former child actor
  - Tamsyn Manou, Australian athlete
  - Chris Sligh, American singer-songwriter and producer (Half Past Forever)
  - Will Solomon, American basketball player
  - Elliott Yamin, American singer
- July 21
  - Josh Hartnett, American actor
  - Justin Bartha, American actor
  - Kyoko Iwasaki, Japanese swimmer
- July 22 – Candace Kroslak, American actress
- July 23
  - Stuart Elliott, Northern Irish footballer
  - Stefanie Sun, Singapore singer
- July 25
  - Louise Brown, British citizen, first human born through in vitro fertilisation
  - Gerard Warren, American football player

- July 26
  - Jehad Muntasser, Libyan footballer
  - Eve Myles, Welsh actress
- July 28 – Hitomi Yaida, Japanese singer
- July 31
  - Will Champion, English drummer for Coldplay
  - Justin Wilson, English racing driver (d. 2015)

August

Andy Samberg

James Corden

Kurt Busch

Kobe Bryant

- August 3 – Mariusz Jop, Polish footballer
- August 4 – Kurt Busch, American race car driver
- August 5 – Carolina Duer, Argentine world champion boxer
- August 6
    - Marisa Miller, American supermodel
    - Freeway, American rapper
    - Peng Cheng-min, Taiwanese baseball player
- August 7
    - Alexandre Aja, French director
    - Vanness Wu, Taiwanese singer
- August 8
    - Countess Vaughn, American actress
    - Natsuko Kuwatani, Japanese voice actress
- August 9 – Daniela Denby-Ashe, English actress
-

- August 17
    - Vibeke Stene, Norwegian rock singer (Tristania)
    - Jelena Karleuša, Serbian pop singer
- August 18 – Andy Samberg, American actor and comedian
- August 19
    - Chris Capuano, American baseball player
    - Qais Al Khonji, Omani Entrepreneur
- August 21
    - Reuben Droughns, American football player
    - Alan Lee, Irish footballer
- August 22 – James Corden, British actor, singer, comedian, and television personality; current host of CBS's The Late Late Show
- August 23
    - Kobe Bryant, African-American retired basketball player (1996-2016)
    - Julian Casablancas, leader singer for The Strokes
- August 24 – Rafael Furcal, Dominican baseball player
- August 25 – Kel Mitchell, American actor
- August 26 – Amanda Schull, American actress
- August 28 – Kelly Overton, American actress
- August 29 – Danielle Hampton, Canadian actress
- August 30 – Swizz Beatz, American record producer and rapper
- August 31 – Ido Pariente, Israeli mixed martial artist

September

Anthony Mackie

Ani Lorak

- September 3 – Tinkara Kovač, Slovenian singer and musician
- September 4
  - ○ Wes Bentley, American actor
  - ○ Frederik Veuchelen, Belgian cyclist
- September 6
  - ○ Mathew Horne, English actor
  - ○ Homare Sawa, Japanese footballer
- September 7 – Devon Sawa, Canadian actor
- September 11
  - ○ Ed Reed, American football player
  - ○ Ben Lee, Australian singer
- September 12 – Ruben Studdard, African-American singer
- September 14
  - ○ Ben Cohen, English rugby union player
  - ○ Carmen Kass, Estonian supermodel
- September 15
  - ○ Eiður Guðjohnsen, Icelandic football player
  - ○ David Sneddon, Scottish singer-songwriter
- September 20
  - ○ Jason Bay, Canadian baseball player
  - ○ Patrizio Buanne, Italian singer
  - ○ Sarit Hadad, Israeli pop singer
- September 21 – Doug Howlett, New Zealand rugby union player

- September 22 – Harry Kewell, Australian footballer
- September 23
  - Anthony Mackie, American actor
  - Worm Miller, American screenwriter, director, actor
- September 24 – Wietse van Alten, Dutch archer
- September 25
  - Jodie Kidd, English model
  - Ani Lorak, Ukrainian pop singer, songwriter, actress, entrepreneur, and former UN Goodwill Ambassador, Eurovision Song Contest 2008 runner-up
- September 28 – Pastora Soler, Spanish singer
- September 29 – Kurt Nilsen, Norwegian singer
- September 30 – Candice Michelle, American professional wrestler and model

October

James Valentine

Usher

CM Punk

- October 2 – Ayumi Hamasaki, Japanese singer
- October 3
  - Christian Coulson, English actor
  - Shannyn Sossamon, American actress
- October 4
  - Dana Davis, American actress
  - Mark Day, Canadian actor
  - Kei Horie, Japanese actor
- October 5
  - Shane Ryan, Irish Gaelic footballer
  - James Valentine, American musician (Maroon 5)
  - Morgan Webb, television personality
- October 9 – Nicky Byrne, Irish musician (Westlife)

- October 10 – Francis Escudero, Filipino congressman, senator (*Chiz*)
- October 14
  - Paul Hunter, English snooker player (d. 2006)
  - Usher, African-American singer and actor
- October 18
  - Wesley Jonathan, American actor
  - Mike Tindall, husband of Zara Phillips, daughter of Anne, Princess Royal
- October 20
  - Kira, German singer
  - Virender Sehwag, Indian cricketer
- October 21 – Joey Harrington, American football player
- October 23 – John Lackey, American baseball player
- October 24 – Carlos Edwards, Trinidadian footballer
- October 25
  - Russell Anderson, Scottish footballer
  - Zachary Knighton, American actor
  - David T. Little, American composer and drummer
- October 26
  - Phil "CM Punk" Brooks, American professional wrestler
  - Antonio Pierce, American football player
- October 27 – Vanessa-Mae, Singaporean violinist
- October 28 – Justin Guarini, American singer
- October 29 – Travis Henry, American football player
- October 30 – Matthew Morrison, American actor and singer

November

Rachel McAdams

Katherine Heigl

Sharmeen Obaid-Chinoy

- November 1
  - Jessica Valenti, American blogger and feminist writer
  - Manju Warrier, Indian actress
  - Mary Kate Schellhardt, American actress
- November 3 – Tim McIlrath, American punk singer (Rise Against)
- November 5 – Bubba Watson, American golfer
- November 6
  - Taryn Manning, American actress
  - Sandrine Blancke, Belgian actress
- November 7
  - Zaheer Khan, Indian cricketer
  - Mark Read, English singer (A1)
- November 8 – Ali Karimi, Iranian football player
- November 9 – Sisqó, African-American actor and singer
- November 10
  - Nadine Angerer, German footballer
  - Kyla Cole, Czech model
  - Diplo, American DJ, music producer, and songwriter
  - Eve, African-American rapper
  - Drew McConnell, English musician
- November 11 – Jyothika, Indian actress
- November 12 – Sharmeen Obaid-Chinoy, Pakistani journalist, activist and filmmaker
- November 13 – Hsu Wei Lun, Taiwanese actress (d. 2007)
- November 14
  - Bobby Allen, American ice hockey player
  - Xavier Nady, American baseball player
- November 17
  - Reggie Wayne, American football player
  - Rachel McAdams, Canadian actress
- November 18
  - Damien Johnson, Northern Irish footballer
  - Aldo Montano, Italian fencer
- November 19 – Matt Dusk, Canadian jazz musician & singer
- November 21 – Annie, Norwegian singer
- November 24 – Katherine Heigl, American actress

- November 25 – Shiina Ringo, Japanese singer and musician
- November 26 – Jun Fukuyama, Japanese voice actor
- November 27 – Mike Skinner, English musician
- November 29 – Ludwika Paleta, Polish-Mexican actress
- November 30
    - Emil Steiner, American author
    - Gael García Bernal, Mexican actor

December

Ian Somerhalder

Nelly Furtado

Katie Holmes

John Legend

- December 1 – Mat Kearney, American singer/songwriter and musician
- December 2
  - Nelly Furtado, Portuguese-Canadian singer and songwriter
  - Christopher Wolstenholme, British multi-instrumentalist (Muse)
- December 5
  - Neil Druckmann, American writer, creative director and programmer
  - Olli Jokinen, Finnish ice hockey player
- December 7 – Shiri Appleby, American actress
- December 8
  - Ian Somerhalder, American actor
  - Vernon Wells, American baseball player

- December 9
  - Jesse Metcalfe, American actor
  - Gastón Gaudio, Argentine tennis player
- December 10 – Brandon Novak, American freestyle skateboarder and TV/radio personality
- December 12 – Monica Bîrlădeanu, Romanian actress
- December 15 – Jerome McDougle, American football player
- December 16 – Joe Absolom, British actor
- December 17
  - Manny Pacquiao, Filipino boxer
  - Chase Utley, American baseball player
- December 18
  - Daniel Cleary, Canadian ice hockey player
  - Katie Holmes, American actress
- December 19 – Patrick Casey, American screenwriter and actor
- December 20
  - Geremi, Cameroon footballer
  - Jacqueline Saburido, Venezuelan-born drunk driving accident survivor and promoter of non-drunk driving
- December 21 – Shaun Morgan, lead singer of South African band Seether
- December 22 – Edo Maajka, Bosnian rapper
- December 23
  - Andra Davis, American football player
  - Jodie Marsh, British model
  - Víctor Martínez, Venezuelan baseball player
  - Estella Warren, Canadian swimmer, model, and actress
- December 24 – Yıldıray Baştürk, Turkish footballer
- December 24 – Paula Seling, Romanian singer and radio DJ
- December 26 – Kaoru Sugayama, Japanese volleyball player
- December 28 – John Legend, American singer
- December 29 – Alexis Amore, Peruvian actress, dancer, and model
- December 30
  - Inferno, Polish musician
  - Tyrese Gibson, African-American actor and singer
  -

- December 31
    - Craig Wayne Boyd, American country music singer and winner of The Voice season 7
    - Eisa Al Dah, Emirati professional boxer

Date unknown

- Fabian Göranson, Swedish illustrator
- Raghda Khateb, Syrian voice actress
- Tomicah Tillemann, American diplomat and social entrepreneur

Deaths

January

- January 1 – S. Poniman, Indonesian singer and actor (b. 1910)
- January 5
    - Wyatt Emory Cooper, American screenwriter and author (b. 1927)
    - Sally Eilers, American actress (b. 1908)
- January 8 – André François-Poncet, French politician and diplomat (b. 1887)
- January 9 – Noble Johnson, American actor (b. 1881)

Hubert Humphrey

- January 13
    - Hubert Humphrey, U.S. Vice President and Senator (b. 1911)
    - Joe McCarthy, American baseball manager (New York Giants) and a member of the MLB Hall of Fame (b. 1887)

- January 14
  - Harold Abrahams, English athlete (b. 1899)
  - Kurt Gödel, Austrian-born mathematician (b. 1906)
- January 18
  - Carl Betz, American actor (b. 1921)
  - Walter H. Thompson, English Scotland Yard detective (b. 1890)
- January 22 – Herbert Sutcliffe, English cricketer (b. 1894)
- January 23
  - Terry Kath, American rock musician (Chicago) (b. 1946)
  - Jack Oakie, American actor (*The Great Dictator*) (b. 1903)
- January 26 – Leo Genn, English actor (b. 1905)
- January 27 – Oskar Homolka, Austrian actor (b. 1898)
- January 29 – Tim McCoy, American actor (b. 1891)

February

- February 2 – Wendy Barrie, British actress (b. 1912)
- February 7 – Keizō Komura, Japanese admiral (b. 1896)
- February 9 – Warren King, American cartoonist (b. 1916)
- February 11
  - James B. Conant, American chemist and headmaster of Harvard University (b. 1893)
  - Harry Martinson, Swedish writer, Nobel Prize laureate (b. 1904)
- February 15 – Ilka Chase, American actress (b. 1900)
- February 18 – Maggie McNamara, American actress (b. 1928)
- February 19 – Pankaj Mullick, Bengali composer and singer (b. 1904)
- February 22 – Ernest Palmer, American cinematographer (b. 1885)
- February 27 – Vadim Salmanov, Russian composer (b. 1912)
- February 28
  - Philip Ahn, Korean-American actor (b. 1905)
  - Zara Cully, American actress (b. 1892)

March

- March 1 – Paul Scott, English writer (b. 1920)
- March 11
  - Claude François, French singer-songwriter (aka Cloclo) (b. 1939)
  - Sofia Vembo, Greek singer and actress (b. 1910)
- March 12 – John Cazale, American actor (b. 1935)
- March 18
  - Leigh Brackett, American author (b. 1915)
  - Peggy Wood, American actress (b. 1892)
- March 19 – Gaston Julia, French mathematician (b. 1893)
- March 20 – Jacques Brugnon, French tennis player (b. 1895)
- March 21 – Cearbhall Ó Dálaigh (Carroll Daly), 5th President of Ireland (b. 1911)
- March 22 – Karl Wallenda, American circus performer (b. 1905)
- March 23 – Haim Ernst Wertheimer, Israeli biochemist, recipient of the Israel Prize (b. 1893)
- March 31 – Charles Best, American-born medical scientist (b. 1899)

April

- April 4 – Semyon Davidovich Kirlian, Russian inventor (b. 1898)
- April 8
  - Ford Frick, 3rd commissioner of Major League Baseball (b. 1894)
  - Lon L. Fuller, American legal philosopher (b. 1902)
- April 9 – Michael Wilson, American screenwriter (b. 1914)
- April 14
  - Joe Gordon, American baseball player (New York Yankees) and a member of the MLB Hall of Fame (b. 1915)
  - F. R. Leavis, British literary critic (b. 1895)
- April 16 – Lucius D. Clay, American military governor of Germany after World War II (b. 1897)
- April 19 – Joe Dougherty, first voice of Porky Pig (b. 1898)
- April 21 – Sandy Denny, English singer (b. 1947)

- April 22
  - Basil Dean, English film director and producer (b. 1887)
  - Will Geer, American actor (b. 1902)
- April 25 – Leo Najo, American baseball player (b. 1899)
- April 27 – John Doeg, American tennis champion (b. 1908)

May

Aram Khachaturian

Aldo Moro

Tamara Karsavina

- May 1 – Aram Khachaturian, Armenian composer (b. 1903)
- May 6 – Ethelda Bleibtrey, American Olympic swimmer (b. 1902)
- May 8 – Duncan Grant, Scottish painter (b. 1885)
- May 9 – Aldo Moro, former Prime Minister of Italy (assassinated) (b. 1916)
- May 12 – Robert Coogan, American actor (b. 1924)
- May 14 – Robert Menzies, 12th Prime Minister of Australia (b. 1894)
- May 22
  - Joe Colombo, American gangster (b. 1914)
  - Aubrey Fitch, American admiral (b. 1883)
- May 24 – Barry Atwater, American actor (b. 1918)
- May 26 – Tamara Karsavina, Russian ballerina (b. 1885)
- May 28 – Arthur Brough, British actor (b. 1905)

June

- June 1 – John W. Burton American film producer, and cinematographer (b. 1906)
- June 4 – Mark R. Shaw, American temperance movement leader and Prohibition Party candidate for vice-president in 1964, (b. 1889)
- June 7 – Ronald George Wreyford Norrish, British chemist, Nobel Prize laureate (b. 1897)
- June 9 – Prince Nicholas of Romania (b. 1903)
- June 18 – Walter C. Alvarez, American physician (b. 1884)
- June 20 – Mark Robson, Canadian film director (b. 1913)
- June 22 – Jens Otto Krag, Danish politician, former Prime Minister (b. 1914)
- June 24 – Robert Charroux, French writer (b. 1909)
- June 25 – Barry Brown, American actor and writer (b. 1951)
- June 27 – Josette Day, French actress (b. 1914)
- June 28 – Clifford Dupont, 1st President of Rhodesia (b. 1905)
- June 29 – Bob Crane, American actor (b. 1928)

July

- July 1 – Kurt Student, Luftwaffe general and commander of the German airborne forces during World War II. (b. 1890)
- July 3 – Edouard Kutter, Luxembourg photographer (b. 1887)
- July 8 – Aagot Nissen, Norwegian actress (b. 1882)
- July 10
  - Takashi Suzuki, Japanese politician. (b. 1882)
  - John D. Rockefeller III, American philanthropist (b. 1906)
- July 14 – Gaston Ragueneau, French athlete (b. 1881)
- July 16 – Howard Estabrook, American actor (b. 1884)
- July 20 – Gerald Warner Brace, American writer, educator, sailor and boat builder (b. 1901)
- July 25 – Helen Corke, English writer (b. 1882)
- July 30 – Umberto Nobile, Italian aviator and polar explorer (b. 1885)

Pope Paul VI

Jomo Kenyatta

August

Charles Boyer

- August 2
  - Carlos Chávez, Mexican composer (b. 1899)
  - Totie Fields, American comedian (b. 1930)
- August 4 – Frank Fontaine, American comedian and singer (b. 1920)
- August 5
  - Dutch Clark, American football player (Detroit Lions) and a member of the Pro Football Hall of Fame (b. 1906)
  - Jesse Haines, American baseball player (St. Louis Cardinals) and a member of the MLB Hall of Fame (b. 1893)
  - Queenie Smith, American actress (b. 1898)
- August 6
  - Pope Paul VI (b. 1897)
  - Edward Durell Stone, American architect (b. 1902)
- August 7 – Eddie Calvert, British musician (b. 1922)
- August 14 – Nicolas Bentley, British writer and illustrator (b. 1907)
- August 16 – Jean Acker, American actress (b. 1893)
- August 21 – Charles Eames, American architect and designer (b. 1907)
- August 22 – Jomo Kenyatta, Kenyan statesman (b. 1894)
- August 24 – Louis Prima, Italian-American singer and actor (b. 1910)
- August 26 – Charles Boyer, French actor (b. 1899)

- August 28
  - Bruce Catton, American Civil War historian, Pulitzer Prize winner (1954) (b. 1899)
  - Robert Shaw, English actor (*Jaws*) (b. 1927)
- August 31 – Lee Garmes, American cinematographer (b. 1898)

September

- September 4 – Mario Palanti, Italian architect (b. 1885)
- September 7 – Keith Moon, English drummer (The Who) (b. 1946)
- September 8 – Leopoldo Torre Nilsson, Argentine film director (b. 1924)
- September 9
  - Jack L. Warner, Canadian film studio founder (b. 1892)
  - Hugh MacDiarmid, Scottish poet (b. 1892)
- September 11
  - Mike Gazella, American baseball player (b. 1895)
  - Georgi Markov, Bulgarian writer (b. 1929)
  - Ronnie Peterson, Swedish Formula One driver (b. 1944)
- September 12 – Frank Ferguson, American actor (b. 1899)

Pope John Paul I

- September 15 – Willy Messerschmitt, German aircraft engineer (b. 1898)
- September 23 – Lyman Bostock, American baseball player (b. 1950)
- September 24
  - Ruth Etting, American singer (b. 1896)

- o Hasso von Manteuffel, German general and politician (b. 1897)
- September 25 – Bret Morrison, American voice actor (b. 1912)
- September 26 – Manne Siegbahn, Swedish physicist, Nobel Prize laureate (b. 1886)
- September 28 – Pope John Paul I (b. 1912)
- September 30 – Edgar Bergen, American actor and ventriloquist (b. 1903)

October

- October 6 – Johnny O'Keefe, Australian singer (b. 1935)
- October 7 – Henry Corbin, French philosopher, theologian and scholar (b. 1903)
- October 9 – Jacques Brel, Belgian singer (b. 1929)
- October 10 – Ralph Metcalfe, American athlete (b. 1910)
- October 12 – Nancy Spungen, American groupie and girlfriend of Sid Vicious (b. 1958)
- October 16 – Dan Dailey, American actor (b. 1915)
- October 19 – Gig Young, American actor (b. 1913)
- October 20 – Gunnar Nilsson, Swedish race car driver (b. 1948)
- October 23 – Maybelle Carter, American singer (b. 1909)
- October 28 – Geoffrey Unsworth, British cinematographer (b. 1914)
- October 30 – Wallace MacDonald, Canadian actor (b. 1891)

November

- November 6 – Harry Bertoia, Italian artist and designer (b. 1915)
- November 7 – Gene Tunney, American boxer (b. 1897)
- November 8 – Norman Rockwell, American artist and illustrator (b. 1894)
- November 10 – Theo Lingen, German actor (b. 1903)
- November 15 – Margaret Mead, American anthropologist (b. 1901)

Harvey Milk

- November 16 – Claude Dauphin, French actor (b. 1903)
- November 18 – Jim Jones, Peoples Temple founder (b. 1931)
- November 20
    - Robert Alan Aurthur, American screenwriter (b. 1922)
    - Giorgio de Chirico, Italian painter (b. 1888)
- November 23 – Jacques Bergier, French writer (b. 1912)
- November 27
    - Harvey Milk, American gay rights activist (b. 1930)
    - George Moscone, American 37th Mayor of San Francisco (b. 1929)
    - Susan Shaw, British actress (b. 1929)
- November 28 – André Morell, British actor (b. 1909)

Golda Meir

December

- December 8 – Golda Meir, Prime Minister of Israel (b. 1898)
- December 10
    - Emilio Portes Gil, 41st President of Mexico
    - Ed Healey, American football player (Chicago Bears) and a member of the Pro Football Hall of Fame (b. 1894)

- ○ Ed Wood, American filmmaker (b. 1924)
- December 11
  - ○ Raúl Alberto Lastiri, 39th (interim) President of Argentina (b. 1915)
  - ○ Vincent du Vigneaud, American chemist, Nobel Prize laureate (b. 1901)
- December 12 – Fay Compton, English actress (b. 1894)
- December 15 – Chill Wills, American actor (b. 1902)
- December 17 – Don Ellis, American jazz musician, trumpeter, arranger, composer and bandleader (b. 1934)
- December 22 – Olaf M. Hustvedt, American admiral (b. 1886)
- December 27 – Houari Boumédiènne, President of Algeria (b. 1932)

Date unknown

- W. E. Butler, British occultist (b. 1898)
- I. K. Taimni, Indian chemist (b. 1898)

Nobel Prizes

- Physics – Pyotr Leonidovich Kapitsa, Arno Allan Penzias, Robert Woodrow Wilson
- Chemistry – Peter D. Mitchell
- Medicine – Werner Arber, Daniel Nathans, Hamilton O. Smith
- Literature – Isaac Bashevis Singer
- Peace – Mohamed Anwar Al-Sadat and Menachem Begin
- Economics – Herbert A. Simon

In the News

Pope Paul VI dies at age of 80.

Worlds Population Estimated at 4.4 billion.

Britain launches the Motability scheme to provide cars for disabled people.

Argentina Wins 1978 World Cup in Argentina.

Space Invaders Launches Craze for Computer Video Games.

Popular Films - Grease, Saturday Night Fever, Close Encounters of the Third Kind, National Lampoon's Animal House, Jaws 2.

Karl Wallenda, founder of the Flying Wallendas, dies after falling off a tight-rope.

Cardinal Karol Wojtyla becomes **Pope John Paul II.**

Three American balloonists make the first crossing of the Atlantic by hot air balloon in Double Eagle II.

Serial killer David Berkowitz, the "Son of Sam," is sentenced on June 12th to 25 years to life in prison.

Public Service strikes in UK causes major disruption to all services.

Indira Ghandi faces fraud charges in India.

India faces it's longest and worst monsoon season in modern times leaving 2 million homeless.

Printed in Great Britain
by Amazon

41239140R00036